WORTHY WOMAN

How To Effortlessly Gain A Man's Respect,
And Why 'Trying' To Get It Won't Work!

Zak Roedde

CONTENTS

WORTHINESS

Many women are not being treated in a way that makes them feel loved, cherished, and protected by their man. Their feelings aren't heard. Their needs aren't met. Their love is not reciprocated. Their boundaries are not respected. Not to the level that they deserve. Not to the level that they need to truly thrive as women. Not even close.

It's extremely easy and convenient to blame the man for this mistreatment.

"Men are selfish"

"Men are pigs"

"Men don't care about women's feelings"

"Men are only interested in sex"

I get it.

I've seen many men treat women poorly.

I've heard of many men treating women poorly.

I've been a man who has treated women poorly.

It is absolutely true that there is much that men should do to step up and lead their relationships as better men. Men need to find their backbone, and their heart, and learn how to properly love and lead their woman. But that message doesn't empower women, it just leaves them waiting for men, or their man, to step up. They might be waiting a very long time.

What if a man's behaviour towards his woman is just a reflection of what she is communicating to him?

What if a man could feel inspired to treat his woman much better, if she changed what she was communicating?

What if there were practical action based steps that a woman could take to communicate in a radically different way?

The truth is, most men are capable of being the devoted masculine leader that a woman needs. A man who leads his relationship, focused on making his woman feel happy, safe, and loved. A man who works on himself diligently to become a better and stronger man for his woman. Wherever a man is in his current level of growth, he can usually be inspired to start showing up as that man. He just needs the right kind of woman to inspire him.

Such a woman needs to be able to communicate two things: The respect she has for herself, and the respect she has for her man. She must be able to do both or she will not be treated in a way where she feels respected as a woman. When she communicates respect for herself, she is showing that she is valuable as a woman. She's a 'worthy' woman. When she communicates respect for her man, she is showing that he is valuable to her as a man. He is a 'worthy' man, to her. He will only feel intense attraction, connection, respect, and devotion to his woman when she is communicating that she sees him and herself as worthy for each other. He will begin taking his job as the devoted leader extremely seriously when she does this. He will begin doing all he can to meet his woman's needs and make her feel as loved and cared for as possible.

A woman communicates that her man is worthy by respecting him as 'the man' in five different ways.

1.   She communicates that she respects him as the leader by submitting to what he tells her he wants instead of resisting

him.

2.   She communicates that she is appreciative of his gifts by receiving him fully and graciously instead of taking his gifts for granted or resisting them.

3.   She communicates that her man is in charge by not 'trying' to get him to do anything.

4.   She communicates that she trusts her man to properly lead by not telling him to stop doing anything.

5.   She communicates that her man is accepted for the man he is by not blaming him for who he is or what he does.

I had an ex-girlfriend who was very much like this. I will be talking about my ex-girlfriend throughout this book because she is a perfect example of a woman who communicates that her man is a worthy man, but doesn't communicate that she is a worthy woman. She was what most men think of when they visualize the perfect feminine woman. She was very warm, sweet, soft, and loving. She respected me in every way possible as a man by letting me lead and receiving my leadership fully. This is of the utmost importance because a man's greatest need is to lead. He must be in charge of a relationship to feel like the man, and his devotion can only come through his leadership. Not by submitting to hers.

The problem with my ex-girlfriend was that she didn't communicate respect for herself. She didn't communicate that her needs and feelings mattered as much as mine did. When a woman doesn't respect herself but shows a lot of respect for her man, she is communicating that she is less valuable than her man is. She is communicating that he is a worthy man for her, and she is an unworthy woman for him. The larger the worth gap is, the less attracted the man will be, and the less motivated he will be to lead to meet her needs. That was why despite my ex-girlfriend having many amazing qualities as a woman, I was not very attracted to her or interested in meeting her needs. If a woman wants to have her needs met and be treated with respect and care, she must communicate that she is just as worthy as her man.

A woman communicates that she is worthy in five different ways too:

1.   She communicates that she deserves devoted leadership by only increasingly submitting to her man when her man is increasingly devoting his leadership to her.

2.   She communicates that she deserves to receive a man's gifts without having to 'do' anything to get them, by staying in the 'receiving' role instead of the 'giving' role.

3.   She communicates that her needs matter just as much as her man's needs by expressing them all openly without holding back.

4.   She communicates that she deserves her feelings to be taken into account by speaking up whenever she feels hurt, anxious, violated, uncomfortable, or any other negative emotion.

5.   She communicates that she is willing to walk away from the relationship if she isn't getting what she needs.

My wife checked all of the boxes when it came to her own self-respect. I will also be talking about my wife throughout this book because she is a perfect example of a woman who communicates that she is a worthy woman, but misses the mark on communicating that her man is a worthy man. I could feel how much she respected herself right away when we met. That was by far the number one thing that made her so different than most women I had met. And it made me feel very attracted to her. My attraction to her early on was through the roof. The attraction started to wane somewhat as she started treating me with less respect as a man as time went on in our relationship. But the loss of attraction wasn't nearly as big of a problem as my suppressed desire to devote to her. I remained relatively attracted to her because I respected her. But I didn't feel devotional to her, because I didn't feel respected in the way I needed to as a man. For a man to feel truly devoted to his woman, she must be treating him with respect as a man.

When a woman respects herself but doesn't show a lot of respect for her man, she is communicating that he is less valuable than she is. She is communicating that she is a worthy woman, and he is an unworthy man. When a woman is communicating that she is more worthy than he is, he may maintain attraction for her, but will have less interest in devoting his leadership to her. The larger the worth gap is, the more disrespected he will feel, and the less motivated he will be to meet her needs.

This was the problem with my wife. She had many amazing qualities as a woman. She communicated that she was worthy. She also believed and felt that I was worthy to her, but she wasn't communicating that in a way where I felt respected as a man. Whereas I believed and felt that she was worthy to me, but I wasn't communicating that in a way where she felt respected as a woman.

Men and women feel respected in vastly different ways. And the sad irony is the way that many women start communicating that they respect themselves is the way that makes a man feel disrespected as a man. Women do this by acting more like a man with their man. When she acts like a man with her man, she is communicating that she doesn't see him as 'the' man. She is communicating that he is unworthy to be her man. The result is that her man will lose interest in being devotional to his woman, which will make her feel disrespected. This leads to the woman acting even more like a man to protect herself and to try to get her needs met, which makes her man even less interested in meeting her needs because he feels even more disrespected. Which makes her feel increasingly disrespected too!

This is an enormous problem that many men and women are experiencing, and it creates unnecessary conflict and hurt feelings for both partners. It seems like women are damned if they do (have self respect) and damned if they don't (have self respect).

But there is a solution.

It is possible for a woman to make a man feel high attraction for her *and* feel inspired to devote his leadership to her. But it will only be possible when she is able to communicate that she is a worthy woman by respecting herself as a woman, and communicate that he is a worthy man by respecting him as a man. Once a woman is able to communicate both of those things, her relationship will transform rapidly. That is exactly what I will show you how to do in this book. I will show you how to become a Worthy Woman, and treat your man like a Worthy Man. That is the only way your man will feel inspired to devote to you.

Throughout this book, I will be talking about my own experiences using some simple stories. I do this to provide real life concrete examples of the principles I discuss in this book, which will help you better understand the shifts you need to make to have the love life you want to have. But this book really isn't about me or the women I discuss. This book is about you, and the patterns you are stuck in which are preventing you from having your dream relationship.

While my experiences in this book are personal, the principles they illustrate about men and women are universal. That has become undeniable after seeing the incredible shifts of my many women clients from doing this work. So while this book may be triggering, don't brush it off as one man's experience or you may miss out on the opportunity to have what you need in your love life.

SUBMISSION

A woman's submission to her man's leadership is a beautiful thing. It is natural and allows flow between a man and woman. Just like a tango dance, the man leads, the woman submits to his leadership. Both dancers benefit. It's how all good and healthy relationships function smoothly. But a woman should only increasingly submit to her man's leadership when that leadership is devoted to her feelings and needs. Such a relationship is healthy because the man's needs get met through his woman's submission, and the woman's needs get met through the man's devotion. The woman is communicating that she is worthy when she submits to her man's devoted leadership, but only if that leadership is devoted to her needs.

A woman will communicate that she is unworthy and doesn't respect herself when she increasingly submits to her man's leadership even if he doesn't lead in her best interest. She submits because she either doesn't believe she deserves better, or she doesn't know how to say 'no'. She submits even if his leadership hurts her. She submits because she is worried about her man losing interest in her if she doesn't. She thinks her worth comes from what her man tells her to do to meet his needs, because she doesn't realize her worth is intrinsic.

Such a woman will communicate that she is unworthy if she continues to increasingly submit to meet her man's needs without equal reciprocation to meet her needs. The more she communicates that she is unworthy by submitting to undevoted leadership, the lazier and more unmotivated her man becomes to meet her needs. He will lack desire because she is not inspiring his devoted leadership by communicating that she is worthy of it. Men do not have high attraction and respect for women who communicate that they are unworthy. Without that attraction, there will be low motivation from the man to devote to his woman.

My ex-girlfriend would have submitted to probably anything I told her to do. Early on in our relationship I told her to come up to spend time with me at my parents while they were gone on a trip. My parents asked me to stay there to look after their animals, so I wanted company. There was nothing wrong with her submitting to that request on the surface, it's when we look at the context that it becomes a huge problem. She drove all the way up there, and I didn't even tell her I'd pay for the gas money. Then she gave me a ride back down, and I once again didn't pay her for the gas money. It was an eight hour drive each way! I didn't even consider her needs or feelings or what might be fair. In my mind, I was just telling her what I wanted, and she was free to do it or not if it was worth it to her. It was worth it to her, because she valued time with me more than she valued her own self-respect.

My leadership was undevoted to my ex-girlfriend. I wasn't focused on fairness or making her happy. I was focused on making sure my needs were met. I didn't try to coerce her to do anything for me that she didn't want to do, but I did tell her to do things for me even though I wasn't interested in reciprocating. It was selfish leadership. My ex-girlfriend submitting to that kind of leadership made me lose attraction for her, and made me even less interested in devoting my leadership to her. I saw her as unworthy, because she communicated that she was unworthy.

A worthy woman submits to her man's leadership when he is devoted to her needs. Submission is a sign of unworthiness when it is done without devoted reciprocation. But it is a sign of worthiness when a man is leading in a woman's best interest. A worthy woman submits to her man's leadership because she knows that he cares about her and her needs. She knows that not submitting is going to make her worse off, because her man is leading with her in mind. He is using his leadership to make her life better. But she will only increasingly submit to her man if he is increasingly devoting his leadership to her needs.

A worthy submissive woman is incredibly attractive to a man. He feels compelled to devote to her because he can feel she is worth devoting to. He can also sense that if he is not devotional, she will not be submissive. He will sense that he needs to give his absolute best leadership if he wants his woman to submit to it. He will not be able to get away with selfish leadership. This understanding comes from his woman's energy, and it motivates him to rise to the challenge and bring his most devoted leadership.

When my wife and I were first dating, she was submissive to my leadership. She came to see me when I told her to, she went along with whatever plans I had, and she would always follow my lead physically and sexually. Over a period of our first year together, she became much more resistant to submitting to my leadership. At the time, I thought that it was because the honeymoon period was wearing off and she was just showing her true colors. But the honeymoon period can last forever with a man and woman who treat each other as worthy. What was actually happening was she was reflecting exactly what I was giving her. I wasn't used to that experience with a woman.

Back then, I was far more self-interested that I am today. My first priority was my own needs and wants, and my wife's needs and wants were second place. That didn't mean I wasn't loving to her. I showered her with physical affection, I spent lots of quality time with her, and I always made sure she was sexually satisfied. But I did those things because I loved giving in that way, it was fun for me. Whereas I had much less interest in meeting her needs if they didn't align with the way I wanted to give her love. Every time I demonstrated that her needs were not as important to me as my own, she subconsciously had less interest in submitting to my leadership. Which is the right response from a woman. A woman should not submit to a man's leadership more than he is demonstrating his devotion.

The problem with the dynamic between my wife and I was that she was not communicating what she needed in the way a man needs to hear it. She was communicating that she was worthy by scaling back on her submission as she realized my leadership was not fully reciprocal. Her resistance and 'nos' communicated her worth. That kept me very attracted to her. She was showing me that her submission was worth something. But she wasn't able to activate my devotion for her because the very act of resisting me to communicate her worth and self-respect, also communicated that she saw me as unworthy. She wasn't respecting me as a man by respecting my leadership.

A woman communicates to a man that he is worthy and respected when she submits to his leadership. A man cannot possibly feel truly respected in a relationship if his woman is resisting his leadership by giving him excuses, saying 'no', and being unreceptive. It will make him feel purposeless in the relationship, without any real sense of responsibility. He cannot devote to her unless his devotion is through his leadership, so if his leadership isn't respected, he won't be able to devote, nor feel the motivation to do so.

To communicate worth, a woman must be willing to scale back on submission if she is feeling a lack of reciprocation from her man. If her man isn't leading to meet her needs, she shouldn't be submitting to meet his. But first she should express how his lack of reciprocation and devotion are making her feel, as vulnerably as possible. She doesn't do it to try to get an outcome, she expresses it because it is the truth of how she feels. That is how a woman communicates to a man that she sees him as worthy and respects him as a man. It is also the only way to know if a man is willing to become more devoted. Only vulnerability without trying to get an outcome will activate his devotion, because his devotion must come through his leadership. If she tries to get an outcome, either overtly (with direction) or covertly (with manipulation), then her man can only submit to her leadership. And he will resist that. That is why vulnerability must be used.

"I feel sad"
"I feel anxiety"
"I feel anger"
"I feel shame"

A woman should wait for her man to lead her to express why she feels that way, and then explain the behavior and dynamic that is creating the feeling.

"Because I spend a lot of time and money to travel to see you whenever you lead me to meet you."

This is demonstrating worthiness as a woman. Only a worthy woman would speak up like this because she knows her feelings matter, and she knows she deserves reciprocation. If this is done vulnerably without any blame or trying to get an outcome, the man now has an opportunity to reflect on his behavior. She isn't trying to change him. She's only expressing how her man's behavior has impacted her feelings. If he starts adjusting his own leadership, he is responding to his woman's self-worth. He is showing her submission is worth something. He is respecting her by adjusting his leadership.

If her man doesn't adjust his leadership, the woman should scale back her submission to a point where there is equal reciprocation. She submits to a point where she is no longer feeling disrespected and unvalued for how much she is putting in, because she is putting in as much as she is getting back. She should never do this vindictively to punish or teach her man a lesson. That would be manipulation, and only unworthy women manipulate, because they don't believe a man will see her as worthy if she doesn't trick him into it. Instead, she should do it because she values herself too much to disrespect herself by submitting to undevoted leadership. It's about her own self respect, not about trying to get her man to do anything.

When a woman scales back her submission, her man may very well become upset and frustrated that his needs aren't being met. He will feel disrespected as a man. But that is not the woman's problem. If he wants respect and to be treated as a worthy man, he must be willing to show respect and treat his woman as worthy too. He only feels disrespected because he was unwilling to respect his woman.

If her man does get upset, a woman can then repeat herself vulnerably, explaining that the reason she isn't doing what he wants is because she doesn't feel good submitting when he doesn't lead in her best interest. No blame. Just expressing from the heart. Her man's only choices are to start leading with devotion, remain emasculated in the relationship with a woman who won't fully submit to his leadership, or leave.

The most likely outcome is that a woman demonstrating respect for herself and also respect for her man in this way is going to inspire him to become more devotional to her. The more he devotes, the more his woman can safely submit further to his leadership while still maintaining self-respect as a worthy woman. The more she submits, the more her worthy man will have an interest in devoting. His increasing devotion will prove to her that she is a worthy woman who deserves respect by having her needs fully considered. The more that this happens, the more she will begin to truly believe that she is worthy. She will go from acting like a worthy woman to truly becoming one.

RECEIVING

In a healthy relationship, the man is in the giving role and the woman is in the receiving role. The giving role is the leading role. The man leads everything, and is always trying to get an outcome. This should ideally include trying to anticipate many of his woman's needs without her even needing to communicate them. Giving her time when she seems lonely, giving her help when she seems stressed, giving her affection and compliments when she seems sad, giving her space when she seems tired, giving her sex when she seems horny. Giving her security and provision all the time. In this dynamic, the man is always trying to get an outcome, and the woman is receiving the outcome he gives her. If he needs or wants his woman to do something, he just tells her what to do, and she 'receives' that by submitting to his leadership. A woman communicates that she is worthy when she doesn't do anything for her man unless he leads her to do it.

A woman will communicate that she is unworthy and doesn't respect herself when she takes on the 'giving' role and puts her man in the 'receiving' role. Such a woman might give her man gifts, backrubs, affection, sex, blowjobs, time, energy, love notes. She will plan and organize things for him, and take him places, with her money. She will be the one to text him, call him, and get into his physical space. Most of this stuff isn't actually a problem if it is through a woman's submission to her man's leadership. But it is a huge problem when her man doesn't ask for it and she does it of her own initiative.

On the surface, a woman who is proactively in the giving

role might sound like a dream come true for a man. Lot's of love, attention, and free stuff without even needing to tell his woman to do any of it? Amazing! But it's not amazing. A man is not attracted to a woman because of all the nice things she does for him. He is attracted to her first and foremost because of how valuable he perceives her to be. He perceives her to be highly valuable when she perceives herself as highly valuable. He perceives her as of little worth when she perceives herself to be of little worth. And a woman who is in the giving role does not perceive herself as worthy.

A woman in the giving role subconsciously believes that she is less worthy than her man. She is trying to close the value gap between her and her man by 'doing' things for him. Somewhere in the woman's mind, the more she does, the more attractive she will become to her man. She is giving because she believes that her worth comes from the things she can give to him. She believes that if only she can do enough for her man, she will get the love from him that she craves. She believes if she stops giving, her man won't be attracted to her anymore. But the opposite is true, it's being in the giving role that makes her man lose attraction for her. Because she is communicating that she is unworthy.

A woman puts herself in an energetically precarious position when she is in the giving role. She will give and give and give, in the subconscious (or conscious) hopes of getting love back in return. But that love is unlikely to come to her in any sizeable amount, because giving to a man demonstrates she is unworthy, and men are not attracted to women that have lower worth than they do. The result is a lack of the reciprocation the woman needs to feel good and loved. This will make her feel increasingly needy for that love and attention, and the more energy she puts into giving to her man without getting anything back, the needier she will become for the reciprocation.

My ex-girlfriend was often in this giving role with me. She would take me to expensive getaways and events. She would cook me meals, give me back rubs, and get in my space without me asking her to do so. She was always doing things to make me happy. She was always trying to anticipate what I needed and how I felt or would feel. There was one wonderful occasion where she took us to a nice retreat up in the mountains. She paid for all of the food and accommodations. She also paid for a special cooking class for us. She organized all of it, and I did nothing.

I went along with it, because I liked free stuff and experiences. I wasn't going to resist her gifts if my laziness was going to be enabled. I always had a fun time with her. But my attraction for her always remained low, because she was communicating that she was unworthy. I was attracted enough to continue seeing her once a week. But I was not even close to attracted enough to spend lots of time with her every week, or do things for her.

A worthy woman does not spend any time in the giving role. She passively receives a man's gifts. She knows she deserves to be in the receiving role. She know she deserves a man's chivalry, his gifts, his love, his sex, his acts of service, his compliments, his devoted leadership. She knows that she doesn't have to 'do' anything to get her man to initiate contact with her by text or phone or in person. She knows that he will do it on his own, because he enjoys spending time with her. She knows that she doesn't have to buy his love or attention by doing things for him without him telling her to. She knows that she is intrinsically valuable just by being her. She can just sit back and receive what her man gives her.

That doesn't mean a worthy woman is selfish and does nothing for her man. There is nothing wrong with a woman doing lots of nice things for man, she can and should. But only if he tells her to do those things. If she is doing things for her man through her submission to his devoted leadership, then she is showing her worth. But if she is doing it of her own initiative, then she is leading. She is in the giving role. And that is where the man should be. A man is always in the giving role with a worthy woman. He is leading everything, and he is giving his leadership to meet her needs. Because she is worthy of his devotion.

When a woman stays in the receiving role, she is demonstrating her worth. She is communicating that just 'being' is good enough, and she doesn't have to do anything extra to be valuable to her man. This will cause her man to become very attracted to her. He will want to do things for her to make her feel even more valuable, because he sees her as valuable.

My wife was very good at staying in the receiving role in our relationship, because she knew her worth. She knew that she was worthy, and she knew that she didn't have to earn my attention or love. She didn't do nice things for me to make up for a lack of her own perceived self-worth. She stayed in the receiving role. If I wanted her to do something for me, I had to tell her.

Two weeks after meeting my wife, I went out of my way to buy her a 'promise ring'. I walked all over to find a pawn shop and found a cheap but nice looking ring. When my wife came over that night, I 'proposed' to her, and asked her to be my girlfriend. I did that because the idea of giving her that experience and gift filled me up with joy. It was a little silly, but also very meaningful. I don't take commitment lightly, showing my commitment to her through such a display was a huge deal.

My wife didn't have to 'do' anything to get that commitment. She would come see me when I led her to do so, and she just got to enjoy the ride. She just got to be herself, because she knew being herself was good enough for any man. It was sure good enough for me. Her being herself was good enough for me to want to spend my life with her, because she communicated that she had so much self-worth. And I wanted that in my life forever.

The problem with the dynamic between my wife and I was that she was in the receiving role, but usually could not fully feel or show appreciation for my gifts similar to how she did with that promise ring. A man's gifts include everything he gives her. His

16

attention, his compliments, his humor, his affection, his acts of service, his time, his energy, his advice, his leadership, his love. Everything that a man is, is a gift to his woman when it is given.

Often when I would give her many of these gifts, she wouldn't even show any happiness at having received them. It felt like I was meeting her expectations rather than giving her gifts, and so I lost a lot of interest in giving gifts. When I did give gifts, I focused only on what I enjoyed giving, because it was fun for me. I would give her lots of affection, humor, compliments, and attention. But I wouldn't give her what she really needed to feel loved and appreciated, because she had a hard time showing her appreciation. Without his woman being able to show appreciation, a man will lose interest in devoting to her needs.

For a man to feel compelled to give his gifts in the giving role, he has to feel appreciated, he has to feel received. He feels received by seeing how he is positively effecting his woman. The more pleased she is with his gifts, the more received he feels.

A man feels respected and worthy when his gifts have a strong positive effect on his woman's emotional state. He feels worthy because his gifts are received by his woman as if they were very valuable. If he doesn't feel received, then he will feel like his gifts are not valuable to her. If he doesn't feel his gifts are valuable, then he will feel less valuable as a man. He will feel like he is unworthy to her, which makes him feel disrespected and even rejected. To avoid feeling that way, he will eventually stop giving to his woman. It's not because he doesn't love her or value her or respect her. It's because he doesn't feel loved or valued or respected, because he isn't being properly received.

To communicate worth, a woman must stop trying to give anything unless she is led to do it. She just leans back, and stops 'doing'. She needs to let go of the need to control a man's attraction by doing things for him. She just opens herself up to receive instead. This may be very difficult for a woman if her self-worth is based on what she can do for her man. She will feel addicted to being in the giving role, and will feel afraid to stop. She may start to feel anxious that she will lose her man, or that he will get angry at her.

Both of those things are possible, but what is more likely is that her man will start to become more attracted to her. The more she leans back and stops giving, the more she communicates that she is worthy. By stepping out of the giving role, she is no longer putting more energy into the relationship than she is getting. She will no longer feel a neediness for reciprocation, because she is no longer giving. Her neediness will go way down, and it will give her man energetic space. The more she does that, the more her man feels attraction for her, and the more he desires to take on the giving role and give to her.

Once a woman is able to lean back and stop giving, her next step is to learn to receive well. A woman who leans back but can't receive all of a man's gifts with appreciation is communicating that she is worthy, so her man will feel attraction for her. But she is not activating his devotion, because he doesn't feel like she sees him and his gifts as worthy. He will lose interest in trying to devote his leadership if she isn't showing that she is receiving those gifts fully with appreciation. For a man to feel motivated to devote, he needs to feel received.

The reason many women have difficulty showing appreciation for a man's gifts is often because of high expectations going unfulfilled or barely met. That was the issue with my wife. But for many women, the reason is because they don't feel worthy to receive those gifts. Same lack of appreciation, for completely different reasons. Such a woman believes that she is unworthy of a man's gifts, but what she is communicating to her man is that *he* is unworthy to give those gifts to her. That is the message he receives. He ends up being the one that feels unworthy and disrespected, when really it was because of his woman's own feelings of lacking worth.

The best way to start learning how to receive and show appreciation as a woman is to use "I feel" statements. The purpose of these statements is it helps a woman connect into her heart to feel, and then express the feeling in the most vulnerable way. All she needs to do is move her attention to her heart when a man gives her something, and fully feel the emotion it creates in her. Then verbalize it.

"I feel so happy right now."
"I feel excitement."
"I feel free and joyful."

The more a woman connects to her heart and learns to feel and show that feeling, the more she will be able to show the appreciation for her man on her face, her body, and in her energy. It's not just the words. What really matters is the energy. The words just help get a woman's heart out of her chest, and onto her sleeve. The words act as a gateway for a woman to relearn how to feel, and express the feeling.

As a woman is able to increasingly receive and show her appreciation, the more her man will want to step further into the giving role and do more for her. The more he gives, the more she receives. The more she receives, the more she realizes that she is worthy and deserves what she is getting. Her man's actions start to prove to her that she is worth it, just by letting go and being herself. Without trying to 'do' anything to get that love.

NEEDS

In a healthy relationship, a man and woman will both have needs. Needs are anything that a person requires to thrive and feel fully loved, supported, and valued. Common needs that a woman has in a relationship is to be able to fully trust her man, to feel safe to express her feelings, to feel fully seen and heard, to feel desired, and to feel loved. There are a wide variety of ways that each of these needs can be met depending on the individual woman. What one woman needs isn't necessarily what another woman needs. Being able to properly express needs is of critical importance for a woman to be able to do. If needs are not expressed, they will almost certainly not be met. A woman communicates that she is worthy when she can express her needs directly and without apology. She knows her needs matter, and she knows they deserve to be met.

A woman who stays silent or tries to get her needs met indirectly through manipulation or hints is communicating that her needs do not matter. She is communicating that she is unworthy, because deep down she believes that she *is* unworthy. She perceives that her needs will be a burden to her man. She has a fear that if she expresses them, he may not want to stay. Or that he will ridicule her needs, or will not take them seriously. She stays silent or expresses indirectly because she is trying to subconsciously close the perceived worth gap. On some level, she believes if she doesn't burden her man with any of her needs, her worth will go up in his eyes, and he will stay attracted to her.

The exact opposite happens. When a woman doesn't voice her

needs, the damage is two-fold. First, her needs are unlikely to be met, because her man is not a mind-reader. This may make her feel sad, unvalued, and needy. This is tragic because she may very well be with a man who would want to meet her needs, if only he knew what they were. Because he doesn't meet her needs, she ends up strengthening her belief that she doesn't deserve her needs to be met.

But the second problem is that her silence will communicate that she is unworthy to her man. This will lower her man's attraction for her. The less she speaks up, the less attracted her man will be. He is getting an increasingly clear sense of how little she values herself as time goes on without expressing her needs. This will act as a snowball effect where the less she communicates, the less interested her man will become in meeting her needs, and the less her needs get met. Which will make her even less confident in expressing her needs.

My ex-girlfriend wouldn't ever speak up when her needs were being unmet. I don't even think she was conscious of what her needs were, because those needs were deeply suppressed. In our entire relationship, I do not recall her ever voicing what she needed to be happy, or what was making her unhappy. Since she didn't voice her needs, I didn't offer to meet them. My mind was completely unfocused on what she might need, because her silence communicated that what I was giving her was enough. Whenever we were together, I would only be focused on what I needed.

There was one point in our relationship where my ex-girlfriend started asking me questions about why I never texted her throughout the week when I wasn't with her. I told her it was because I don't like texting. She continued to ask a bunch of questions trying to understand me better. But never once did she actually express that she had a need for me to stay in contact with her. Nor did she express that she felt sad or unvalued when I didn't try to stay in contact with her. In hindsight, I realize that she did have such a need. She likely needed that to feel secure and valued. But she didn't have the confidence to voice that need.

A woman who is worthy will always express her needs. She expresses them because she knows that her needs matter, she knows that they deserve to be met. Her needs are just as important as her man's needs. She knows that she would be disrespecting herself if she didn't speak up when she has a need, so she always expresses herself, even if it makes her uncomfortable.

When a woman expresses her needs, it communicates to her man that she is worthy. He will be much more likely to feel that her needs matters, because she believes they matter. It is a self-fulfilling prophecy. The more worthy a woman is, the more a man will feel compelled to meet her needs when they are expressed. Self-worth creates attraction, and attraction creates desire in a man to give. He will want to give more time, more energy, and more resources to meet her needs.

My wife always expressed her needs with me. I never had to wonder if she needed something, because if she did, she would tell me. She was always direct and no-nonsense about it. She was aware she had needs, and she knew they deserved to be met. She voiced them fearlessly and confidently.

My wife and I always texted each other a lot when we were away from each other. Usually many times a day. I discovered with her that I do love texting, only if I am attracted enough and interested enough in the woman to feel compelled to do it. But one night I went out to a party alone, I was having so much fun by four in the morning that I didn't think to text her. And when I did think of it, I didn't do it because I didn't want to wake her up. When I got home, she was really upset that I didn't text her to let her know everything was fine, and she wasn't shy about telling me. She made it extremely clear that she had a need that was very important to her. She was direct and firm telling me what she needed. That was how she always was when expressing her needs.

It was very clear that she was worthy.

The problem with the dynamic between my wife and I was that she was communicating that she was worthy and respected herself by expressing her needs, but she wasn't communicating that she saw me as worthy and respected me as a man. Whenever a woman tries to lead her man in any way, she is communicating disrespect. She is taking on his role as the leader and trying to get him to submit to her leadership to meet her needs.

A woman is leading whenever she tries to get any kind of outcome with a man. This can be direct and obvious like when a woman nags or bosses a man around. It can also be covert through manipulation to lead without a man knowing that she is in charge. But it can also be subtle and kind and respectful "Hey could you please text me when you know you will be staying out late." This is leadership, and while it is respectful communication in most human interactions, it is disrespectful to a man when it comes from his woman. Because he must always be leading to be properly respected. If his woman tries to get an outcome with a directive question ("Can you do X?") his only choice is to say 'no' or submit to that leadership.

A man is not going to feel good about meeting his woman's needs by submitting to his woman's leadership. His greatest need in the relationship is to lead, and be respected as the man in that role. If his woman tries to lead him in any way, he will not feel respected, and he will not want to give her what she needs. Not because he doesn't care about her, but because he doesn't want to submit to her. He will only feel compelled to devote to his woman's needs if he is able to do it through his leadership, not through his submission.

That was exactly the problem with the dynamic between me and my wife. I was still quite attracted to her and saw her as a worthy woman, but I had a low interest in meeting her needs. Instead when she tried to get her needs met, it would often create a conflict. They would sometimes be met, and sometimes not, but neither of us would feel good about it. I didn't like submitting to her leadership ever, and she didn't like how resistant I was to meet even her smallest needs through her leadership. She didn't understand why I was so resistant, and at the time, neither did I!

A woman should not try to become worthy by learning to lead her man to meet her needs. It will never work well. Even if she does develop the belief that she is worthy, most men will not treat her as worthy. Only weak approval seeking men will treat her well, because they want her approval, and they are willing to submit to get it. If developed men do submit to meet a woman's needs through her leadership, it's only because they care about her. They know the 'right thing' is to meet her needs and not neglect her, but that doesn't mean they enjoy doing it.

A woman becomes worthy by realizing that her needs matter. Her needs are just as important as her man's. They should be expressed. But they should be expressed without her trying to get any outcome from her man. She should only express the problem she has, rather than expressing the solutions she wants. She expresses for the sake of expressing, rather than assertively directing. Like an artist painting a masterpiece, she paints because she needs to express, not to get something out of it.

"I can't do this." (Vulnerably expressing an inability to do something.)

"I need some space." (Vulnerably expressing the need, not assertively directing her partner to meet it.)

"I feel sad." (Vulnerably expressing the feeling that is caused by the need going unfulfilled.)

"Can I talk to you?" (Vulnerably asking permission to do something that she needs/wants.)

These are the only ways a woman can express her needs in a

way where she is still respecting her man as worthy, because she isn't trying to lead him to do an outcome. After reading these examples of communication, you may be thinking that none of this sounds like something a worthy woman would say. Perhaps you think it sounds weak and dis-empowered. You would be very sorely mistaken. It would be very weak if a man communicated in this way. But this is exactly how a worthy woman would express her needs to her man.

A worthy woman would know that her man would *want* to do his absolute best to meet her needs and make her happy. She would have no need to assert herself and try to direct her man to meet her needs. She knows that all she needs to do is express what her problem is, and her man will jump to the rescue as her hero. Not because she is defenceless, helpless and weak. But because she is radiant, priceless, and worth devoting to. Her needs matter so much that she doesn't even need to *try* to get them met.

The more a woman expresses her needs in this way, the more a man will feel devoted to meet them. He will want to meet them without her trying to get him to do so. The more a man does this, the more it proves to her that she really is worthy. Only a worthy woman would have a man want to meet her needs without her trying to get them met. The more she develops her belief in her worth, the easier it becomes to express her needs without trying to get an outcome. She develops the trust that she doesn't need to put in *effort* to get her needs met.

FEELINGS

A woman must recognize that her feelings are extremely important, and she deserves a man who cares about how he is making her feel. When his behaviour is causing her to feel sad, angry, scared, insecure, unloved or any other negative emotion, she needs to speak up. A worthy woman will always speak up when her man is doing something that hurts her feelings, because she knows her feelings matter, and she doesn't deserve to feel that way.

An unworthy woman will allow her man to make her feel bad. She allows herself to be treated like a doormat, with her man wiping his dirty feet onto her. She will put up with her man yelling at her, calling her names, breaking promises, lying, cheating, and even being physically abusive. She allows it, because subconsciously she believes she is worth very little. She believes if she doesn't let it go, her man will get upset, or will leave, or she will have to leave. And she doesn't want that. She values her man more highly than her self-respect.

When a woman allows her man to make her feel bad, she is communicating that she doesn't deserve respect. She is communicating that she doesn't have any worth that needs defending. She is communicating that her feelings do not matter. When a woman doesn't express herself after being hurt, she is doing it to subconsciously stay attractive to her man. She believes that if she were to speak up, her man would lose interest in her, or would spend less time with her. Or she believes that if she were to speak up, she would get a bad reaction from him, and that it's best to avoid that.

But whatever a woman's reason is, her silence is communicating that it is acceptable to treat her poorly. If she tolerates being treated like garbage, she will be valued like garbage. And men are not attracted to garbage. Of all the ways that a woman can communicate that she is unworthy, this one is the most effective.

I never did something as terrible as lying or cheating or calling my ex-girlfriend names. I was not an abusive person. However for most of my life, I was a very inconsiderate person. This became most apparent when I moved in with my ex-girlfriend for a while. She invited me to stay with her rent free when I was staying with another friend. I took her up on the offer. I ended up staying with her for months. The entire time I almost never cooked, and I was messy and rarely cleaned up after myself. I acted as if I had no responsibility to be considerate to her feelings at all.

There was one time when I was living with my ex-girlfriend when I was talking to her in a very condescending way. She didn't say anything about it. She just continued talking to me as if nothing happened. And as if it didn't even bother her. What she was really doing was giving me permission to treat her that way. Through her silence, she was communicating that it is acceptable to talk to her without respect. I didn't often do it, because I know its not nice to do, but she was communicating that her worth was so low that it was fine if I did do it. She was communicating that she was a doormat.

A worthy woman would never allow herself to be mistreated and say nothing when her feelings get hurt. Because she knows exactly what she is worth. She knows that her feelings are of the utmost importance. She will have a very low tolerance for disrespect, and will speak up immediately. She knows that she would be disrespecting herself if she didn't say anything, and she respects herself far too much to do that.

When a woman speaks up and doesn't let a man get away with disrespectful behavior, she is communicating that she is not a woman to be messed with. Her ability to speak up tells the man that she has a lot of worth, so he better take her feelings seriously. This will cause the man to become far more attracted to her, because he can feel her worth.

My wife was such a woman. I have never met a woman who takes her boundaries as seriously as she does. There was nothing I could do to make her feel bad without me immediately hearing about it. She would tell me when I broke my word, when I raised my voice, and when I talked to her in any kind of way other than respectfully. I haven't ever hurt her feelings by doing something extreme like being physically abusive or cheating. But I am pretty sure I would get divorce papers if I ever tried. I can feel how seriously she values herself, and so I feel compelled not to do anything that devalues her.

I have had the exact same situation with my wife that I had with my ex-girlfriend. I have talked to her in a condescending way. Never on purpose, but sometimes I was not fully aware of how I was acting. There was never a time where she didn't speak up and tell me what I was doing. There was never a time where she did that where I didn't take her seriously. I could feel how serious she is.

The problem with the dynamic between my wife and I was that she was communicating worthiness, but she was doing it with her leadership. She would set boundaries and tell me to stop doing something, to prevent herself from feeling bad. Setting boundaries is when a woman leads a man to stop doing something by saying "don't", "stop", or "no". Or by telling a man that his behavior is inappropriate with the implied intent of leading him to change. I tried hard not to cross her boundaries by being disrespectful, because I respected her. This respect kept me attracted to her. But the very act of her enforcing boundaries also stopped me from feeling devoted to her, because it felt disrespectful. I was being treated as an unworthy man.

Whenever a woman leads a man, it is disrespectful and communicates that she doesn't see him as worthy. Even when leading him to stop violating a boundary. Telling a man "don't", "stop" or "no" are all forms of leadership. She is telling him what to do (or what not to do) to try to get him to submit to her lead. It is a woman's right to do this if she really wants to. If a man is purposely violating a boundary without regard for how she feels, it is perfectly reasonable and encouraged to do it. It's far better than saying nothing at all. But most of the time, there is a far superior way for a woman to communicate that she is worthy, which also communicates that her man is worthy. To do this, she must express how she feels when her man crosses her boundary, ideally by using an "I feel" statement. As vulnerably as she can. Whatever the feeling is that she is experiencing, that is what should be expressed.

"I feel anger"
"I feel anxiety"
"I feel shame"

The focus is only on the feeling so that a woman can tap deeply into her heart and feel what she is experiencing. Once she has done so, she should wait for her man to lead to ask why she feels that way. Then she should express exactly what behavior the man exhibited to cause the emotion. She shouldn't judge or label the behavior as bad or wrong or inappropriate, because that is also received by a man as a form of disrespect. She just describes the behavior that is causing her to feel that way, without trying to get any outcome.

The act of voicing her feelings and explaining them communicates that a woman has worth. Only a woman with self-worth would communicate her feelings. If she didn't value her feelings, she wouldn't communicate them. She doesn't express them assertively, trying to force her man to stop doing what he is doing because she feels a certain way. All she is doing is showing him what his behavior is doing to her. Because a worthy woman knows that she doesn't need to enforce boundaries with her man, she knows that her man will care enough about her feelings to change his behavior without being told to do so.

Only by expressing her feelings will a woman give her man the respect he needs to feel compelled to take responsibility for his actions as an act of service to his woman. If he values his woman and is devoted to her, he will stop what he was doing, without being told to do so. He will work on creating his own inner boundaries for his behavior, because he doesn't want to hurt his woman. He will choose to alter his behavior because of his love for his woman, rather than because his woman won't let him continue the behavior. A man feels compelled to be better for a worthy woman, without her trying to get him to be better.

But for a woman to truly be worthy, she must be willing to do something if her man demonstrates that he isn't interested in setting his own boundaries for his behavior. She values herself too much to expose herself to disrespect for any length of time. She expresses her feelings as vulnerably as she can. But if her man continues to be disrespectful, she sets boundaries for herself. She doesn't tell him his behavior is wrong and she doesn't tell him to stop. She just sets boundaries for herself for her own protection of her heart, her body, and her possessions.

"I need to be by myself to process my feelings right now." (When her man doesn't stop talking disrespectfully even after she told him what she is feeling.)

"I can't lend you my car anymore." (When her man doesn't take care of it even after she told him she feels unvalued.)

"I'm going to go home." (When her man spends his time on his phone even after she told him that she feels disrespected.)

"I'm going to spend the weekend by myself." (When her man was rude to her and didn't apologize, and she still feels hurt.)

She doesn't tell her man to stop talking disrespectfully. She doesn't tell her man to treat her car with respect. She doesn't tell her man to put his phone away. She doesn't tell her man to not come over to see her. She just expresses her feelings, and if he doesn't care about how he is effecting her, she sets a boundary for her own behavior and states it out loud. She leaves him to deal with the consequences of his disrespect. She doesn't do it to manipulate, she does it because she values herself and how she feels so highly.

The more a woman expresses how she feels (and is willing to set boundaries for her own behavior if her man doesn't care), the more her man will start to develop inner boundaries for his behavior. He will start to act in a way that takes her feelings into account. He will start to see that it is his responsibility to act in ways that make his woman feel good and avoid acting in ways that make her feel bad. The more he does this, the more it will prove to his woman that she is worthy. She does deserve to be treated in a way where her feelings are considered as important.

LEARNING TO WALK AWAY

The ability to walk away from less than you deserve is the most important aspect of being a worthy woman. A woman could learn to submit only to increasingly devoted leadership. She could learn to lean back and receive and stop giving to make up for a lack of self worth. She could learn to express all of her needs. And she could learn to express her feelings whenever her man does something that hurts her. But if she isn't fully willing to walk away from less than she deserves, none of those other actions that communicate worth will make a significant difference.

A woman is unworthy if she is unable to walk away from a man who doesn't treat her as worthy. Her inability to walk away trumps everything else she does to communicate that she is unworthy. It isn't the actual walking away that matters. It's the ability to do so. When a woman doesn't have the ability to walk away, she holds herself with weak energy. Her energy will be more needy when she submits, receives, expresses needs, and expresses hurt feelings. A man will feel her dependence on him. He will feel that he's 'got her' and can do no wrong to lose her. And so regardless of how she tries to communicate her worth in other ways, it will all be empty of real meaning.

If she isn't willing to walk, it's all just talk.

My ex-girlfriend did eventually walk away from me. I had left many of my belongings at her home when I left to travel central america for a few months without her. We were non-exclusive at the time, so sometimes I would just up and leave. When I came back, I needed a place to stay. She told me to take my bags and leave, I couldn't stay there. I was confused, and asked her why not. She told me that I wasn't considerate of her feelings and that she didn't like how that made her feel. I was annoyed that she had this newfound respect for herself. But I also respected her more because of it. More importantly, she respected herself more because of it. She had taken one step forward to becoming a worthy woman.

A woman's self respect must be infinitely more important than any man. It must always be prioritized. If a woman isn't getting what she deserves from a man, she removes herself from his life and finds a man who values her properly. She will find a man who makes her feel happy, loved, cherished, cared for, respected, secure, and worthy. But before she removes herself from her man, she should continue showing him full respect as a man. Her respect for him should never waver. If she doesn't communicate full respect to him as a man, she will never truly know if he isn't treating her well because he doesn't respect her, or because she isn't communicating respect for him.

But her respect for herself should never waver either. Maintaining respect for herself and for her man is the best shot a woman has at inspiring her man to grow up and begin devoting his leadership to her. That is when a man is most likely to start putting a lot more effort into becoming a better leader for her. But if he doesn't, she must be willing to walk away. No exceptions. If a man doesn't start growing up when a woman is doing everything to communicate that she is a worthy woman and he is a worthy man, nothing else she does will help. Her only option is to walk away, and she must walk away. If a woman continues to tolerate less than she deserves, she'll continue to get less than she deserves. She'll also prove to herself that this is what she deserves, because it is the best that she'll ever get if she is unwilling to walk away.

Once a woman makes the choice to no longer tolerate less than she deserves, she will be committed to leaving men who don't treat her well. This mindset shift is what will change her love life. Men will respond to her differently because she is proving to herself that she does have worth. The proof is in the action; only women with self-worth will easily walk away from less than they deserve. Every time a woman does this, she further proves to herself that she has worth.

The amazing thing about doing this is that the action changes how a woman feels about herself. Her self worth goes up. She will start feeling like a worthy woman. Walking away from mistreatment acts as the ultimate affirmation. Preferably before it starts to get bad. This will change a woman's belief about herself so that she holds herself differently. She starts increasingly feeling like a woman with high self worth, because she is a woman who acts like she has high self worth. The change in how she feels will start attracting better men, and it will start inspiring men to treat her better. As men treat her better, she will start to see that she deserves that better treatment. Her belief in her worth becomes stronger the more that men treat her the way she deserves.

When I met my wife, her self-worth was very clear. I could tell that she would walk away if I didn't treat her well. She didn't have to say it. I just knew it. I could feel it. And I felt very attracted to her because of it. I knew that I couldn't take her for granted, because I knew she would be willing to walk away if I treated her poorly.

But we also ended up in a stalemate. She remained very attracted to me, and I remained very attracted to her. We both had high respect for each other as *people* and saw each other as worthy *people*. But she wasn't treating me like a worthy *man*, and I wasn't treating her like a worthy *woman*. It wasn't because we didn't respect each other. But we weren't communicating that respect properly. She didn't understand how to communicate respect to me as a man. And I didn't understand how to communicate respect to her as a woman. We just didn't understand how different men and women really are from each other. Like most couples, we were ignorant.

My wife didn't want to walk away because she (for the most part) felt respected as a person. But she also wasn't fully happy in the relationship because she didn't feel respected as a woman. When a woman isn't fully happy in a relationship, her natural tendency will be to *blame* her man for her feelings. Which was exactly what she did to me.

A woman is blaming when she is energetically trying to force responsibility for how she feels onto her man. This will usually come with attempts to rationalize him as 'bad' or 'wrong'. Subconsciously she is trying to convince her man that he is bad or wrong. If he will accept the blame, she can then feel better. "You are selfish and that is why you don't care about my needs or feelings". This is usually the narrative that a woman is trying to convince herself and her man to believe.

This is certainly what my wife tried many times. But it didn't 'work'. It only led to conflict every time where very little ended up getting solved. A man is not going to accept a woman's blame, because he is not responsible for how she feels. He is responsible for his own behaviour, but not how his behaviour emotionally effects his woman. He may choose to adjust his behaviour because of how it impacts his woman, but if he does, it must come from his freedom to choose. He must choose to change his behaviors as a gift to his woman, to make her better off. Rather than do it because of the burden his woman put on him through her blame.

Whenever a man is blamed for hurting his woman in any way, he will feel disrespected. Blame is always communicating disrespect because it is an energetic attack. It is also communicating disrespect because the woman is assuming that her man doesn't care about her feelings, when usually that isn't the case at all. Usually a man hurts his woman's feelings out of ignorance or because he feels disrespected as a man, and doesn't know what to do about it.

When a woman blames a man, the last thing he will want to do is change for her. He would be disrespecting himself if he did. He would be communicating that he is unworthy, because he is accepting responsibility for something that is not his responsibility to take. He is also accepting his woman's abuse rather than setting a boundary and putting a stop to it, which is further communicating that he is an unworthy man. Any man that does accept blame is weakening the relationship by disrespecting himself, and any woman who blames is weakening the relationship by pushing her man away or energetically 'forcing' him to change for the wrong reasons. Nothing good can ever come from blame.

A woman should make one of two choices with her man. She should either walk away because he isn't treating her as well as she wants or deserves, or she should stay in the relationship and accept and love her man for exactly who he is right now. Flaws and all. Immaturity and all. A man needs to feel fully accepted for who he is to have any desire to change. If he feels like his woman thinks he is not good enough the way he is, he will dig his heels in and refuse to change if he believes he is worthy. Whereas he will change himself to get his woman's approval if he really believes he is unworthy, which will only lower his worth further. The change won't be real or long-lasting because it's all done for approval.

If a woman chooses to stay in the relationship, she needs to commit herself to accepting her man exactly how he is. She needs to commit to not trying to change him, and not blaming him for not being the way she would ideally want him to be. Instead, she should get her attention off of her man, and put her attention on working on herself. She should focus on learning to simultaneously communicate that she is worthy and that her man is worthy. She should not do any of this to *try* to change her man, because that would be manipulation. Her purpose of changing herself should not be to get an outcome from her man. It should be because she wants to work on herself. She should be working to become better for herself. And she must act on faith that her man will eventually work hard to reflect her own changes.

These are the man ways a woman should be working on herself:

1.　She respects herself by not submitting to her man when he is not leading with devotion. She respects her man when she vulnerably expresses how his leadership is emotionally effecting her, and explains that is why she is not submitting further.

2.　She respects herself by getting out of the giving role and into the receiving role. She respects her man by learning to receive his gifts graciously with vulnerable appreciation.

3.　She respects herself by speaking up about her needs. She respects her man by speaking up about her needs by vulnerably expressing the problem (which can be her feelings) or asking permission rather than trying to lead him to meet those needs.

4.　She respects herself by vulnerably expressing when her man's behavior effects her. She respects her man by not leading him to stop doing something, and if she has to protect herself as a last resort, she sets boundaries for her own behavior.

She doesn't try to change her man, she only tries to change herself. If at any time she decides that her man is not willing to do the work to reflect her own changes, she has one more thing she must do to communicate that she is worthy:

5.　She respects herself by walking away from the relationship. She respects her man by not blaming him for his

37

behavior and trying to get him to change.

A worthy woman who respects her man doesn't try to change him and doesn't try to blame him. She just accepts him, loves him, but chooses to walk away.

Because she knows she deserves better.

CONCLUSION

I led my wife to communicate respect for me as a man, I taught her the very things I am teaching you in this book. I simultaneously led myself to communicate respect for her as a woman. I showed her how to treat me as a worthy man so that I would feel compelled to treat her like a worthy woman.

If I had known what I know now, I could have led my ex-girlfriend to communicate respect for herself. I could have shown her how to treat herself as a worthy woman, so that I would also feel compelled to treat her like a worthy woman. (not that I have any regrets, I'm very thankful with how things turned out)

If women learn the communication tools in this book, they will transform themselves, and inspire their men to transform themselves.

If men learn the communication tools in this book and lead their woman to use them, they will transform their women, and in the process of devotional leading, they will transform themselves.

Relationships get a lot more fun and fulfilling when both partners treat each other, and themselves, with the respect that they deserve.

But making these shifts will not be easy. In fact, it will almost certainly be the hardest thing you ever do. Even if you now have a general idea of what you need to do. There's a few reasons for that.

1. It's very uncomfortable. Letting go of control as a

woman, or taking control as a man may go against all of your learned survival patterns. The level of discomfort and number of excuses you make to stay stuck will keep you avoiding what you really need to do.

2. It's very painful. On this journey you will be judged. Your needs will often not be met. This process will also take far longer than you likely anticipate. When you don't get the responses you want, the pain and stories you tell yourself will compel you into giving up.

3. You will make tons of mistakes. I've outlined the basics in this book to get you started and give you a fantastic overview of how to create the dream relationship and shift your communication. But there is a steep learning curve and the only way to get what you want and need is to make thousands of mistakes along the way.

4. You won't know how to communicate in every situation. There is far more depth to this work than what I have outlined here. I'd need to write a thousand books of this size to fully convey the depth and breadth of communicating as a man and woman. While it is theoretically possible to figure it all out by trial and error like a good social scientist, the three points above are going to make that far more challenging than it needs to be.

I do have solutions for these problems though, because I want to make this journey as easy as I can for you.

SOLUTION 1: Join our facebook group. With over 10,000 members, you get to be part of a huge community who are learning from my books and teachings. It's FREE.

SOLUTION 2: Read all of my other books. They all contain different pieces of the puzzle to make these shifts easier for you. The more you understand conceptually, the less mistakes you will make and the less likely you will be to give up.

SOLUTION 3: Join our 2 hour Polarized Communication Masterclass. We don't just talk about masculine and feminine communication, we demonstrate it in live roleplays. You also get to ask us questions. Seeing this in action will supercharge your understanding of what this looks like energetically and it will be a powerful belief shifting experience.

SOLUTION 4: The first three solutions are easily affordable (or in the case of the group, free). But if you know you want real expert support at helping you make these shifts, join us in my group program for men and for women; 'Relationship Of Your Dreams Academy'. This is where you will get all of the video content you need to understand what and how to shift on a far deeper level. You will get a group of hundreds of dedicated clients to ask questions, have this communication role modelled, and practice communicating in a safe supportive container. You will also get one on one and group roleplay calls where we will roleplay any relevant situations to show you how to make these shifts and lovingly correct you when you misapply the teachings.

The Academy is focused on giving you the space to practice and refine your communication and learn to receive, while we support you in your journey. We help you move through your pain, your fears, your stories, and your many inevitable mistakes. We take you on a journey from understanding this work conceptually in your head, to understanding it and shifting it in your body. We facilitate your embodiment.

The Academy is more than a coaching program. It's a family. My family, that I created.

Working with us doesn't mean we can take your fear away or make this journey painless. That would be impossible. But we can take you by the hand and make it a lot easier for you.

We can decrease the amount of time that these shifts would take. The same progress you would make in many years to a decade could be made in a matter of months or up to a year. We will help you through all of your fears, and self-sabotage, and make this considerably less painful, and significantly more fun than it would be alone.

It's possible to do it all yourself. I would never lie to you and say it isn't. But you'll be paying a very heavy price in time and an unnecessary degree of painful feelings." After all, if you're a mountain climber, you could climb Mt. Everest by yourself. But with a competent team of sherpas who've got your back and show you the way with their decades of expertise, why would you attempt Mt. Everest by yourself? It would be lonely, cold and potentially deadly.

We have helped facilitate the transformations of so many men and women so that they could create the relationship of their dreams. I'd love it if you were one of the next ones.

To access any or all of the four solutions presented, go to **www.relationshipofyourdreams.com**

You must choose that you are worth this support to get all that you want out of your love life.

And you are...

.... One last thing. I would be incredibly grateful if you did me favor to fulfill my purpose in helping people transform their relationships: If you found this book helpful, please take two minutes to write a quick review on Amazon. Tell all of your friends to get the book too.

Thankyou for reading.